W9-CAJ-182

Stay Safe Online

# Social Networking and Social Media Safety

### Eric Minton

PowerKiDS press™

New York

Published in 2014 by The Rosen Publishing Group, Inc.
29 East 21st Street, New York, NY 10010

First Edition

Editor: Amelie von Zumbusch
Photo Research: Katie Stryker
Book Design: Colleen Bialecki

Photo Credits: Cover Stephen Simpson/The Image Bank/Getty Images; p. 4 ZouZou/Shutterstock.com; p. 5 iStockphoto/Thinkstock; p. 6 1000 Words/Shutterstock.com; p. 7 Raywoo/Shutterstock.com; p. 9 Goodluz/Shutterstock.com; p. 10 Jose Luiz Pelaez Inc/Blend Images/Getty Images; p. 11 Kamira/ Shutterstock.com; p. 12 Jon Kopaloff/Film Magic/Getty Images; p. 13 Image Source/The Agency Collection/Getty Images; p. 15 iStockphoto/Thinkstock; p. 17 Juriah Mosin/Shutterstock.com; pp. 18, 21 Catalin Petolea/Shutterstock.com; p. 19 Monkey Business Images/Shutterstock.com; p. 20 Andresr/Shutterstock.com; p. 23 MachineHeadz/E+/Getty Images; p. 24 bikeriderlondon/ Shutterstock.com; p. 25 Maartja van Caspel/E+/Getty Images; p. 27 Monkey Business/Thinkstock; p. 29 Peredniankina/Shutterstock.com.

Library of Congress Cataloging-in-Publication Data

Minton, Eric.
Stay safe online : social networking and social media safety / by Eric Minton. — First edition.
      pages cm. — (Stay safe online)
   Includes index.
   ISBN 978-1-4777-2933-5 — ISBN 978-1-4777-3019-5 (pbk.) —
ISBN 978-1-4777-3090-4
   1. Social media. 2. Online social networks—Safety measures. 3. Internet—Safety measures.
   I. Title.
   HM741.M56 2014
   302.23'1—dc23
                                    2013018237

Manufactured in the United States of America

CPSIA Compliance Information: Batch # W14PK2: For Further Information contact Rosen Publishing, New York, New York at 1-800-237-9932

# Contents

Using Social Media ............................................... 4

Choosing Sites ................................................... 6

Getting Started .................................................. 10

Identifying Yourself ............................................. 12

Watching Your Words ............................................. 16

Playing Games ................................................... 20

Bad Behavior .................................................... 22

Dangerous People ................................................ 26

Looking Forward ................................................. 29

Be Smart and Safe ............................................... 30

Glossary ........................................................ 31

Index ........................................................... 32

Websites ........................................................ 32

A social network is a group of people who know each other, such as your extended family or your classmates at school. Online social networks are made up of people who use the Internet to stay in touch. These networks can include thousands or even millions of people, most of whom don't know each other directly.

You can use a computer, tablet, or smartphone to connect to an online social network.

The kids you went to camp with make up a social network of people you know in real life. You can use social media to stay in touch with them during the school year.

Social media are forms of electronic communication. You can use social media to chat with people directly. You can share your ideas and opinions. You can also post messages, photos, and videos to show the people in your social network what's happening in your life. You can even read messages from your friends and family to see what they're up to.

# Choosing Sites

People use social networking for many reasons. Some want to stay in touch with friends and family who live in other states or cities. Others hope to find an online community that shares their interests. Luckily, there are many social networks and social media websites, each serving its own purpose. For example, people often use Facebook to share photos with family members.

Twitter is a microblogging service. People use it to get or spread short snippets of news.

Social media sites also give people places to express themselves. **Blog** sites, such as WordPress, are great places to share stories. Flickr lets you post photographs and drawings. Other sites, like Tumblr, let you share several kinds of things.

**Forums** are designed for conversation. Some are for talking about whatever you want, while others concentrate on specific **topics**, like movies, video games, or sports.

If you love your pet poodle and you want to take good care of it, you might consider visiting online forums about dog care.

New social media sites are developed every day. No one has time to use all of them. If you just want to stay in touch with friends who already use social media, join the same sites they are on. For example, if a friend who is moving away is on Kidzworld, you might want to join it to stay in touch. Otherwise, shop around for social media sites that have features you'll want to use or that focus on topics that interest you.

Many social networks, such as Facebook, Instagram, and YouTube, require users to be at least 13 years old. These sites regularly delete the **profiles** of kids who are under the age limit. Never lie about your age to create a profile.

You can use social networking to connect with people who live across the world or those who are sitting in the same room as you.

To join a social media site, you must agree to that site's rules. These are also known as the **terms of service**. Terms of service are often written in complicated language. Ask a parent to help you understand what the rules are.

Do not tell anyone other than your parent or guardian your password. Even telling your best friend is a bad idea.

When you are thinking about joining a social media site, look over both the site and the terms of service with a parent or other trusted adult.

You'll also need to choose a **user name** and a **password**. These let you safely access a website. Make sure your password isn't something anyone else can guess. It should be something you can remember, though.

Anyone who knows your user name and password can pretend to be you. If someone does something bad using your **account**, you'll be blamed. To keep your account safe, never tell anyone your password. Don't write it down in a spot where someone might find it either.

**11**

# Identifying Yourself

Once you join a social network or social media site, you'll need to set up your profile. This lists the facts about you that anyone else using the same network or social media site can see. Since anyone can look at it, you don't want it to have too much personal information. The most basic part of your profile is your user name.

Consider making up a user name that reflects your interests. For example, if you are a fan of the TV show *iCarly*, you might call yourself iCarlyFan.

In much the same way that a name tag does, your user name and avatar introduce you to strangers.

Each person on a site has to have a unique user name. Do not use your real name as your user name. Most profiles include a small picture called an **avatar**. An avatar also appears next to your posts, making it easy to recognize who is writing. Express yourself with an avatar that shows something important to you, such as a pet, your favorite TV character, or a picture you drew.

## Did You Know?

User names are often just one word. Never use your own name as a user name or a picture of yourself for your avatar.

13

Listing your interests in your profile makes it easier to connect with classmates who like the same things you do. It's good to include things like your favorite group or kind of music, sports teams, books, and TV shows.

On the other hand, you shouldn't share anything in your profile that can help a stranger learn who you are and where you live. This includes your real name and your age. Leave out your home address, your phone number, and the name of your school, too.

Some sites have **privacy settings** that let you choose who can read the information in your profile. You'll want to limit this to people who already know you.

Never include anything in your profile that strangers online could use to figure out where you live.

Online networks and social media sites offer several ways to share what you're doing, thinking, and feeling with friends and family. Email is one way to do this. Replying to posts in online forums is another. **Chat rooms** let you talk to people in real time. Instant messaging programs, such as Pidgin, do, too.

Some forms of communication are public, while others are fairly private. Social media networks often allow for both public and private messages. Always think about whether you want what you are writing to be public. Your support for a sports team is probably fine for anyone to see. However, plans for your birthday party are best discussed in private messages.

Social media is a great way to show off your artistic side, whether you make music, write stories, draw pictures, or do crafts.

## Did You Know?

Check any photos and videos you are planning to post online for hidden clues to your location, such as street signs, landmarks, or a T-shirt with your school's name on it.

Don't include any information that strangers could use to figure out where you live in your public posts. This means never sharing pictures or videos of yourself, your home, your school, or anything else that people could use to find you. Your writing shouldn't include your name or the names of people you know. Don't mention the names of streets or other place names near your home, either.

Digital cameras and cameras in phones make it easy to take photos and post them online. Therefore, you should always think carefully before posting a photo.

If you have a great photo of yourself with your grandparents, share it with them privately. Don't post it in a place where anyone could see it.

Be as careful when chatting online as you are when posting. Never tell a stranger your real name, home address or neighborhood, or where you'll be at a specific time. Never send strangers photos of yourself. If you really want to meet someone in person, ask your parents for permission and have them come with you. People aren't always who they claim to be online.

## Did You Know?

Be careful when someone recommends you visit a website or asks you to download a file. Either one could mess up your computer by giving it a virus.

19

# Playing Games

Online games range from versions of simple board games like Scrabble to those involving imaginary worlds like Whyville, Poptropica, and Club Penguin. Some are free to play. Others cost money to buy or require a **subscription fee** that you pay every month.

There are thousands of different online games. Do you have a favorite?

It's easy to spend too much time playing games online. Talk to your parents about making a schedule that makes time for both online games and other activities.

You can buy things in some online games. For example, you might be able to buy equipment that makes the character that you play in a game a better fighter. The extras that you can buy in an online game often don't cost much. However, these small sums can add up quickly. It's easy to spend a lot of money this way. Always get your parents' permission before you buy anything online.

## Did You Know?

Over 90 percent of kids between the ages of 8 and 11 years old play online games.

Bullying isn't just shoving someone on the playground. Cyberbullying is bullying that happens online and by text message. It is just as bad as being mean in person. It can also get you in real trouble.

Don't insult, embarrass, or scare people, even as a joke. Don't lie or pretend to be someone else. Never make up or spread rumors about other people. Don't share private conversations or other personal information without the other person's permission. It's not okay to do these things even if someone else started it.

It can be hard to do the right thing and not be a bully when your friends are being mean to someone. However, if your friends make fun of someone online, don't join in.

Sending bullying text messages will hurt the person who gets them. At some schools, it will also get you detention. It can even get you suspended or expelled.

23

If someone bullies you, it's not your fault. You're also not alone. About half of all kids get bullied online, and 10 to 20 percent are bullied regularly.

Never respond to online bullies. Instead, set up your account to block messages from the people who are bullying you. You should also report bullies to a **network administrator**. If things get really bad, you can get a new profile, email address, or phone number to make it harder for bullies to reach you.

It's normal to be upset when a cyberbully picks on you. Remember it's not your fault, though.

If you have been cyberbullied, talk to an adult. The adult will be able to help put an end to the cyberbullying. Discussing your feelings will make you feel better, too.

If you're bullied, don't keep it to yourself. Tell a grown-up you trust. Keep copies of every hurtful message people send you to prove that you were bullied.

Online predators are older people who befriend children in order to hurt them. Very few people you meet online are predators, but you can never know for sure if a stranger is telling the truth about who he is.

Predators try to win your friendship and trust with compliments, encouragement, and gifts. They may then start inappropriate conversations, send you personal pictures, or ask you to meet in person. Your parents can help you find out if the person you're talking to is a friend or a predator.

Remember that attracting a predator's attention isn't your fault. If a predator threatens to tell your parents about things you've said or pictures you've sent or received, you should tell your parents yourself instead.

> If you get a message that makes you feel uncomfortable, do not respond to it. Instead, show a parent or other trusted adult.

## Did You Know?

A 2006 study found that 16 percent of kids between the ages of 8 and 19 learned that someone they had talked to online was an adult pretending to be younger.

Other people will always be able to read things you write online. If you erase a post or even delete your profile, people can keep copies of your posts on their computers. Meanwhile, **archive** sites make permanent copies of things online that anyone can view.

Remember that it's not just your friends who read the things that you post. Parents, teachers, and coaches see them, too. Years in the future, people looking to hire you for a job or let you into college will be able to read what you post today. Treat everything you ever say online as public, no matter how private you think it is.

Social media sites provide a fun, helpful way to stay in touch with friends. Use them carefully!

What are your favorite social media sites? Do you prefer playing games, connecting with friends, or sharing your artwork?

# Be Smart and Safe

**1.** Don't join too many different social media sites. Keeping up to date with several sites at once takes up lots of time and energy.

**2.** The size of your social network isn't a competition. Don't worry if people you know have more online friends than you do.

**3.** If someone posts something that makes you angry, calm down. Just because that person is being mean doesn't make it right for you to be mean, too.

**4.** To reduce the risk from predators, never use a camera or voice chat while playing online games.

**5.** If someone asks you to send him an inappropriate picture, tell your parents immediately.

**6.** If someone you talk to online makes you feel uncomfortable or scared, trust your instincts. Stay away from that person and alert your parents.

**7.** If you think something you want to post could possibly embarrass you in the future, don't post it.

# Glossary

**account** (uh-KOWNT)  Something that a business supplies to a person who regularly uses its services.

**archive** (AR-kyv)  A place where records are kept.

**avatar** (A-vuh-tahr)  An image that stands for a person on a website.

**blog** (BLOG)  A place for people to report their thoughts or findings on the Internet.

**chat rooms** (CHAT ROOMZ)  Online places where people can type messages to each other.

**forums** (FOR-umz)  Places to discuss questions of public interests.

**network administrator** (NET-wurk ed-MIH-neh-stray-ter)  A person who is in charge of making sure an online network is working smoothly.

**password** (PAS-wurd)  Letters or numbers used to get access to an account.

**privacy settings** (PRY-vuh-see SEH-tingz)  The way to choose who can see different parts of your profile or posts on social media sites.

**profiles** (PROH-fy-elz)  The facts people share about themselves on social media sites.

**subscription fee** (sub-SKRIP-shun FEE)  Money paid every month to have access to a product or service.

**terms of service** (TURMZ UV SIR-vis)  The rules for users of a site.

**topics** (TAH-piks)  Subjects.

**user name** (YOO-zer NAYM)  The name a person uses to log in to and use a website.

# Index

**A**
account, 11, 24

**C**
classmates, 4, 15
communication, 5, 16

**F**
family, 4–6, 16
forms, 5, 16
forums, 7, 16

**G**
group, 4, 15

**I**
Internet, 4

**M**
message(s), 5, 16, 22,
     24–25

**N**
network
     administrator, 24

**O**
opinions, 5

**P**
password, 11
photos, 5–6, 19
privacy settings, 15
profile(s), 8, 12–13,
     15, 24, 29

**S**
school, 4, 15, 18
social media, 5, 8
social network(s),
     4–6, 8, 12, 30
subscription fee, 20

**T**
terms of service, 10
topics, 7–8

**U**
user name(s), 11–13

**V**
videos, 5, 18

# Websites

Due to the changing nature of Internet links, PowerKids Press has developed an online list of websites related to the subject of this book. This site is updated regularly. Please use this link to access the list: www.powerkidslinks.com/sso/sonet/